The Red Files

Lisa Bird-Wilson

NIGHTWOOD EDITIONS

2016

Nightwood Editions
P.O. Box 1779
Gibsons, BC VON 1V0
Canada
www.nightwoodeditions.com

COVER DESIGN: Angela Yen
TYPOGRAPHY: Carleton Wilson

Black and white cover images:
The General Synod Archives Anglican Church of Canada

Nightwood Editions acknowledges financial support from
the Government of Canada through the Canada Book Fund and
the Canada Council for the Arts, and from the Province of British Columbia
through the British Columbia Arts Council and the Book Publisher's Tax Credit.

This book has been produced on 100% post-consumer recycled,
ancient-forest-free paper, processed chlorine-free
and printed with vegetable-based dyes.

Printed and bound in Canada.

CIP data available from Library and Archives Canada.

978-0-88971-316-1 (paper)
978-9-88971-067-2 (ebook)

THE RED FILES

Dear once and future kin:
kisâkihitin

Contents

*The road we travel is equal in importance to the destination we seek.
There are no shortcuts. When it comes to truth and reconciliation,
we are all forced to go the distance.*

—Justice Murray Sinclair,
Chair of the Truth and Reconciliation Commission of Canada,
to the Canadian Senate Standing Committee on Aboriginal Peoples,
September 28, 2010

I

Mourning Day

these braids remember the women

trembling clump of girlflesh
eyes cast down and away
unfamiliar now
to one another
they mourn the loss
of their hair
                         dropped
like so many laments
clipped connections
to mothers, kohkums or aunties
who greased and wove
the glossy braids
with steady brown fingers

fat braids remember
cry like useless ropes on the floor
the girls long, at least
to step over them
in quiet ceremony
women-power mimicry
to mark the passage
a final regret

but cruel teachers clack
                         heathen
and refuse to appreciate

these braids remember the women

Mischief

Miss Spencer arrives on a Friday by train
a tissue tucked in her sweater sleeve
her suitcase in one long hand, the vision
to civilize clutched carefully in the other

the farm instructor brings the truck
she folds her tall self neatly
onto the passenger seat like an origami bird
allows herself to be jostled
up the bumpy road to the school

it's fair to say she starts with zeal
and a bundle of good will
but soon finds her expectations dashed
salvation more ephemeral than real

for two years she lives at the school
and takes photos of the little girls' class
they come out in sepia tones, their
everyday dresses brown or beige
shapeless sacks like paper bags of loneliness

later, when Miss Spencer has the pictures developed
she's surprised: the aura that surrounds
the girls not nearly as melancholy
as she remembers; instead,

there's some mischief in the little girls' smiles
and the light is bright in the sky—
eyes squinted, hand to brow
Miss Spencer tries to picture them all

After Summer Holidays

first day back at school
barefoot, with summer-worn knees
Tommy Bird
running in the schoolyard
halted; seized
hands on
by Miss Wilkinson
the nôtowêsiw
who smells like cheese
and old coats

she smiles at him like a kind
wolf, and twists him
to face the camera
a hungry glint in her
eye, teeth
breathlessly bared

Tommy's slender shoulders
pinched
in her long fingers

the sun in Tommy's eyes

Boys' Class Date Unknown

frost-breath escapes; any day
everyone expects first snow
each boy has a poppy pinned
to his left lapel, above the heart, reminder
of the Great War
their faces clear
cheeks like glass beads

the Reverend Canon Atwater spends
considerable time setting it up:
the younger boys kneel
in the spiky November grass
despite their good suits
the older ones, support crew,
form a zigzag line behind

a latticework fence the backdrop that almost hides
the brick of the school
burned to the ground in '29

as the shutter clicks Freddie Bird tucks
his head down and forward
hands clutched together in front,
laughter in his chest,
while Alex Moosemay grins out of his skin
face turned
to greet the prairie sky

little Hector on the other side of Freddie,
his one knee forward, chin tilted up
anxious, as if he wants in
on the joke
or might tell

I'm telling you now
it's November
1927, that time
they shared a laugh
those boys
at the school beside the blue sloughs
in the heart of the Touchwood Hills

Girl with the Short Hair

if I wanted to describe the girl to you in a poem I might say the short-haired one but they've all got short hair and she's more than that anyway not just a part of the girls' class making yet another snowman or in dry summer hanging out near the single tire swing looking bored with something clutched in front of her smock, one hand holding it while the other hand plucks at whatever it is, grass or a flower   she's not only a part of this but a "break away," an individual   she has a name but history hasn't recorded it   the curly-haired girl then? surely there must be something better but really they're all so uniform in their black and white photos oversized winter coats sloppy cotton self-sewn dresses and smocks

more like the one with the easy stance left shoulder dropped carelessly as if in this restless time of year she might turn at any moment and run—but it's not what you think, it's not to run away from the school like the others but because it's in her bones to lope under the prairie sky to slap her feet down on the long grasses and across the short weeds that stretch endlessly for miles in all directions   now this is more like it   there she is, the breathless one   the one with the wind-knotted hair

Miss Atwater's Class

hats askew and mitts bejewelled
with snow, coats open
to the weather, the girls play
in the shadow of the school, just inside
the invisible fence line
they make snowmen and snowwomen
while a huddle of trees holds watch

the girls' class grows up in nine years
of sharp-edged photos, each time exposed
after play, exhausted—
in the front row an unwavering eye
catches the camera, an Indian
girl, number One-
Seven-Four on the school roll call
the girl with a narrow look, small
for her age, straight-faced,
never smiling, never
frowning, unreadable
as if she willed her young self long
ago to stop scenting the trap line, smoked
hide a vivid memory, pushed
aside: dense sage,
wild root, the open plain

Métis

Métis road allowance squatters
with their raw camps set up on the edge
of the exact reserve boundary, she sees them all
the time, those kids, school-less, she sees
those half-breed kids who look no different
from herself and her friends, sometimes

in spring, every single thing
they own fits in the wagon pulled
by the one sapless horse, away
for summer work, or back
from winter trapping

her mother says something nice
about the half-breed boy, the one
who comes to the house to visit
and have tea with sugar and sometimes a crust of bannock
she likes him and her mother says he is
a good boy

but then one day in the not-work or trapping season,
he disappears
him and his whole family are moved
away and other families evaporate too
in the middle of the night
shacks burnt into the dirt and raked clean

her mother helps her
understand people
can just disappear
like that
like the seasons or the wind
she says, *we are all
impermanent* and when the girl looks puzzled
mother says *like melted candle wax or snow* and then
it's finished: *what are you doing inside,
go out and play*

on the empty road, fingers of sunlight
comfort her back and her shoulder flesh;
she runs to feel her own quick breath

Grasshopper

in the shadows between two school buildings, the residence and the
rectory, she lies on the ground on her belly, head on crossed forearms,
the threat of June heat menacing the air while tricky grass quivers at
her ankles

minutes ago she had the wind knocked out of her; the smile erased
off her face

she back-hand wipes her nose and a grasshopper jumps nearby, deftly
she cups her hand over it

its head pinched between thumb and forefinger, she draws down the
grasshopper's L-shaped foot: flex and bend, flex and bend

the mechanical knock-knee: convincing and in her guts a stirring
faith that all things are made perfect by god

somewhere on the road a car horn sounds, a sign, surely, of something
she hops to her knees then her feet, tosses the grasshopper
onto the flattened grass

squatting she prompts its rump with her finger,
it twitches, draws in a delicate leg
jump, she demands and when it does not
she rises and lifts her foot
to extinguish the evidence
with her bare sole
the car blasts again from the road
she turns and runs to see who has come

This Day

the Cree child, kâ-nêwonâskatêw's grandson, works
at perfecting his one hard line
on the board: *I will not speak Indian anymore*
one hundred times

and the girl with the shy smile makes hand stitches
tiny staccato notes a cryptic code no one can crack
white thread on white cotton apron invisible
messages for each girl to carry close to her heart as she works
from one side of her day to the other

Miss Blinkensop and her camera set to capture the mundane
moments as obscene as the sun through the south window

Baby Thomas coaxes a smile out of the headmaster's wife
bangs his chubby fists on the table, tripwires her severity
when he grabs her hand in his strong baby grip
and pulls it to his mouth

a boy learns to steal: objects, valuable or not;
food, always valuable; glances; and best of all girls
off into a corner

Clara tells Ernestine her secret and they smoke
leaf and grass cigarettes
pinch each other's cheeks red
and wait for something else to happen
besides a bell or getting caught

Blood Sisters

between learning and laundry
backs against redbrick building
legs crossed Indian-style
Agnes tells Leona
"you should marry my brother"

they pinky swear
but it's not set
until Agnes swipes
a kitchen knife
and they pledge in blood
to be sisters forever
pressing their palms together
a sticky red promise

teacher catches them out
of sight behind the rectory
pulls their hair
flushed and inflamed
she pinches their legs
to hear them squawk
makes Agnes kneel
to lick Leona's hand wound
a viscous curious bloom
clean before sending them
to scrub floors
on prayer-bruised knees

Baby Thomas

in his winter journal he writes about the baby that has come to the school to stay: "Baby Thomas" they call him he is so well and truly alone in this world   his father brought him to us shortly after the mother died then the grandmother   we could see by the way he was desperate with the squint around his eyes and the state of his clothing very nearly rotting off him the baby I mean but the father too all the children in fact had been wearing their clothing all the summer and it was disintegrating under the dirt and grime right in front of our eyes   headmaster agreed   at first baby cried every day but soon he began to learn the system of bells   a bell rings to tell the children when to rise when to wash dress eat go to class work play sing sleep... I feared Baby Thomas would be crushed by loneliness as I have seen so many succumb to but the headmaster's wife decided to make a pet out of Thomas our baby and everyone was then given permission—or so it seemed—to baby the child to give him affection and special treats   he has become our collective project and slowly he has turned out happy much to our great delight when he smiles or laughs or shows affection thankfully he is not sullen like the older children can be

Farm Instructor

afternoon chores and the sun
is three hours past its highest point
hot on their dark heads they seek the shade
behind the big barn, the boys
four of them including Ronny
decide to take their chance to run
and on a silent cue
they take off

across the open grass and down the slope
breaking through tree branches
shadow dappled panic
hearts beat faster than chased rabbits
skinny legs push for home
boughs cracking toward light and a chance
wordless spirited breaths follow
one another

and the farm instructor inside his house
boots off, already drunk
in his chair by the south window, dreaming
sun-warmth on his forearm and right thigh

and when he hears about the boys he releases
a heavy sigh
stiff with the beating he'll give
the one he catches first
he laces his boots and sends the hand for the truck
hopes to be back before dark

it'll be Ronny who feels the rough hands
of the farm instructor
pull him easily to the ground
heavy knee on his narrow chest
the breath crushed from his lungs
as he steels himself to be beaten
like a man

The Finest in the Dominion

Saturday is his day to take
a boy. Mostly they are all the same
to him, but this Saturday it's Kenneth,
the most recent
quiet lad to be seduced
by a promise
of driving the school bus.

Here I call him Kenneth, but to name him
is the challenge, when his has only been
a number
but I will call him Kenneth
and while we are naming, I dare you to cite
a single ten-year-old
boy any one out of hundreds
who would be able
to resist, able to measure
the price of that first joyride.

What he did was this—
offered the boy, Kenneth, the chance
to drive the big school bus.
But here's the rub:
Kenneth in his principal's reach
he's too small to touch
the pedals and the
steering wheel at once
so he sits on the headmaster's
lap. Don't think Kenneth hasn't heard
the other boys calling
him the principal's fag baby
but he, too young to really

understand those words,
went along anyway with the man
whose single-mindedness and hard
work built the school residence
to one of the finest in the dominion.

Tunnel

restless rumours spur
spirited schoolboys
along an idea
thinking itself real:
a secret tunnel
rooted under redbrick
coupling school and chapel
                         anarchy
rousing stripling thirst
every boy's dream
to penetrate
the dark passage

secretly they search
for that labyrinth—
every square inch
of the school
probed for entry:
they seek, not light
through a crack, but an opaque portal
into deeper darkness

a bold-faced boy lies
claims to have seen
that place, the tunnel
lying in wait
together the boys imagine
a red road unseen
by a cold blue eye
an Indian underground prepared
for their traffic and the ricochet
of their unbroken soprano voices

"Within the Circle of Civilized Conditions"

in dormitory room 204
on the second floor
twelve-year-old Charles or Charley
or Bobby or fourteen-year-old Hector
and Donald and Mike
                     one boy
who is many in a repeating shell game,
the boy whose prayers all reach
for home
his moshum and tobacco lake
instead shakes the memory
from his skin
of hands
unwelcome
when he was ten and drew the attention
of his teacher; now
the only way he knows how
to remove that touch,
he hangs
himself
with a rough leather belt
against his antler-velvet skin
he hangs himself
crooked
from the metal shaft of his bunkbed
he hangs himself
from the showerhead
he hangs himself
from the railing between the stairs
he hangs
his hungry body
to weigh heavy
on his birdbone neck

Beside a Residential School

kohkums dig
their crooked fingers
earth-deep
in remembering

like overgrown children
they scrape
in a twenty-foot square
garden plot
hunched on their haunches
they till the soil

small buttons, from school
uniforms, unearthed
alongside bantam bones

imagine: boys on one side
girls on the other
sent to slumber without
a goodbye
in unplanned
graves, their hide
coverings long ago
melted away
into clay

while grandmothers search out
lost children,
nearby, the Elders
lightly drum
singing the spirits home
a handful of buttons and bone

II

Standard Features

she visits the site of the razed school
on top of the hill
where her kohkum attended
and the kohkum before her
expects nothing; finds instead

two items, saved
on demolition day
and later cast in concrete

first, the school bell
once with the power to tell everyone exactly what to do
here now only to vex— grounded
to drop sharp remembered notes
that leave their mark

second, the tortured rock
headstone from the top of the school, relic
of another time, bears the date *1929*
and embodies all the silence: listen

a hawk screams overhead
weeds grow in patches near the remains
and their gravemound placement, on top of the hill
unsheltered from the cold, brings shivers
and if she stands still long enough
wind-tears to the eyes

Black-Eyed Susan

Indian summer sunny Rebecca
picks the flowers
wild from the side
of the roadway, like her father
did once to give to her mother
whom he called his black-eyed Susan
making her blush and brush
her hand at him, *awus*
a gentle rebuke
go on
but Rebecca caught her mother
later, when she thought no one
could see, looking at her father
in a tender way, a smile
gracing the corners of her mouth

her mother's fine
fingers snapped the stems
to remove the seedheads
from the stalks, used
the golden blooms, each with its one
big eye, to put in a Player's
tobacco tin centre-stage kitchen table;
set aside the scraggly stems to bruise
or boil later into a catch-all medicine
snake bite poultice for healing
many ills, her gentle fingers
at service, hard used

and so Becca wanders from the school
to pick three hairy stalks
five flower heads nodding
and peaking
like skinny phallic dreams caught
in her fist
under her dress her ribs rub
raw against the hungry inside
of her belly, her legs
lean, like wâpôs in spring
and still she aches for the secret look
her mother gave her father

Indian Preacher

the ladies of the women's auxiliary
sound almost tender
when they write the history of the area
Touchwood
Qu'Appelle
no history would be complete without a reference
to the Indians, they say
as if they must explain the inclusion
apologize for their shortcomings, their failure
to exclude:
the exclusion of exclusion

so they tell about a model of a good Indian
the Christian Indian
preaching the gospel
from Indian Head to Last Mountain Lake
in the field he is a preacher
a kind of teacher and, they say,
treaty four interpreter,
one of the few named Indian men
among countless unnamed
women, men and children of treaty
(naturally the Lieutenant Governor of the Northwest Territories
"presided over" the treaty signing
and he had a name)

the ladies of the auxiliary are full
of wandering footnotes and good deeds
in parenthesis;
proud of their subject, he is
friend of the white man, friend of the government
the Christian Indian Preacher
who kept southern chiefs out of Riel's "rebellion"
the life of the Indian Preacher:
content to travel with his blanket
and tell his fellow Indians
god is love
"a true Indian" he lived
a poor man, died a poor man
surely he will have his reward
in heaven—
that's the way the ladies put it

In 1874 Treaty Four was signed at the Qu'Appelle Lakes after a month of discussion and negotiation. One of the Cree leaders, kâ-nêwonâskatêw, was renamed George Gordon by the government treaty makers after the English poet George Gordon, or Lord Byron, as he was known. The only obvious similarity passed down in the record is that each man, kâ-nêwonâskatêw and George Gordon, had a clubfoot. This has been assumed to be the reason behind the renaming.

kâ-nêwonâskatêw

at the Qu'Appelle lakes
kâ-nêwonâskatêw
he who walks on four claws
speaks long in Cree
inspiring treaty agents
to follow the drumbeat
the swath of red letters
from the back of his throat
words trailing like ribbons
of gravity purling the shoreline—
breeze on water's slow surface

môniyâs ideas drift
like blowing sand toward
spur-marked parchment
each curved X a small dominion
after many hours of double speak

one by one Anglo faces soften
as they circle into sleep by the fire
where they share a dream
about George Gordon, their poet

and when they wake, inspired
they Anglo-name
kâ-nêwonâskatêw for Byron
scandalous and incestuous
bastard son of Mad Jack
retitled more than once himself:
mad, bad and dangerous
a limping devil, *Yes*, they say
George Gordon, they say
nodding their heads, convinced

nearby, kâ-nêwonâskatêw
ignores otisihkân edicts
pale turnips his name for them
unbothered by Anglo oaths
he sets down each solemn token
soberly marking his score
openhanded triplet truths
heroic couplets laid bare
legato fog-swept air

Scrip Buyer 1905

sent from Winnipeg he comes
down the Beaver River
like a fake-bearded pharaoh
ferried in a homemade wooden rowboat
a hard-working hired half-breed at the helm

comes bearing cash in a canvas bag strapped to his hip
steamblotted stinking fabric rubbing
his tender skin raw, drawing up
his coarse-thicket scent
his whole hot body reeking
with purpose yet still somehow
his seems a small menace

he travels for weeks
past river cattails and slippery slick-bellied
mudfish suckling river bottom
to reach Sakitawak
where an upright tent sits,
south side of the nettled bush

where commissioner McKenna holds court
with interior Indians and half-breeds
he questions then christens them
one or the other—declares, names,
classifies, ranks and sorts them
into his doublewide red ledger
to make it all official

on the scrip buyer's first night in camp
with the full moon strung low
against the flat-bottom boats
mosquitoes swarming against their ears:
a handshake
to fix the price this year
at a dollar an acre
for redbacked
half-breed scrip notes

Indian Tallyman

from D.J. Allen, Superintendent Reserves and Trusts, Canada Department of Mines and Resources, Ottawa, ON, December 12, 1941

I think you are familiar

with our plan
of marking beaver houses
every beaver house is staked

just like a mineral claim
placed in charge
of the tallyman

for the group area
in which it is located
the house is numbered

and the tallyman has
in his pocket what is called
a beaver token, bearing

the same number,
the possession of this token,
is evidence
the tallyman can produce

guarantee he is
in fact the man

responsible for the house
the proof being
the marker on the house

bears the same number
as the beaver

token he has in his pocket

In the early 1990s one of the worst known cases of abuse in the history of the residential schools was formally brought to light. It involved one notorious administrator and "hundreds of boys."

Hundreds of Boys—A Response

one hundred
he admits to hundreds
the way the story goes
and so the count is on
each number might break you
each a little boy's name
you say without hurry
voice a tripping drumbeat
every figure a gift
full weight given to each
time to say all hundred:
one minute and forty-six seconds

two hundred
two hundred ten-year-old boys
front the wire fence line
cut through the trees
snake up the hill—
"One Hundred Twenty-Six,
One Hundred Twenty-Seven"—
fold over the ridge
edge close by the saltlick lure
toe-kick it for good measure
curve around old buffalo rock
run their fingertips along his spine
bend past the dry yellow dogwood
and roll down the ravine, tumbleweeds
descending the steep bank, caught in the thickets

here and there, red and ash limbs tangled:
time to count, just three and a half minutes

three hundred
four minutes in and boy Forty-Four
way back at the fence line
pleads with you to stop the count
his dark head is hot
"pîsimowâsis, sun child
switch places with Sixty-Two
he's in the shade of the trees—
some have it easier brother"
but Forty-Four just scowls

stays put

August sun brands his left arm
flies buzz busily with
the stink of Starr in the air
the glare of sun is bright
on the eyes, sîwâstêw
be glad for speaking the truth

more
by five hundred they're stretched
sun-stained, jostling
shoulder to shoulder
past the blue sloughs
down the valley slope
a lengthy run-on sentence
a fierce four kilometres
to the heart of the touchwood hills

"The ██████'s Situation"

To Mr. R. F. Davey, Superintendent of Education, Indian Affairs:

censored: access to information act

Regarding the current worrying situation on the ██████ reserve
school

Over the past two years the school has been the scene of the
following incidents

I

████████ was responsible
for making the girl ███ pregnant
while he was employed by us
and the girl was a pupil
under our care

II

██████████ is sent to jail for tampering
with some of the Indian boy's (sic)
in his charge

III

██████ is fired
for having Indians from the reserve
in her room
in the school at night

IV

██████ runs a mild bootleg establishment
on school property—
he served two terms in jail for drunkenness

V

████ becomes pregnant

████████ is fired

and threatens, "it will all come out then"—

that is, the sort of place we have been running

will then become common knowledge

he goes just the same

VI

aided and abetted by ████

one of our teachers, ████████,

sleeps with his son

each morning ████ lets her back into the school

about 5 a.m.

using his key to the boiler room to let her in

other nights his son gets into the school

up the fire escape

and stays with ████████ all night in her room

████████ knows all about it

VII

████████ brings ████████

back to ████████ and leaves

leaves it with ████████

after which ████████ ████

████ ████ and makes no bones about

████████ █ ████

Reply from Mr. R.F. Davey, Superintendent of Education, Indian Affairs:

after a thorough and exhaustive investigation
I have found
no evidentiary evidence

rather
this most insidious
type of propaganda
has caused confusion
in the minds of the Indians

as you know
Indians are very poor witnesses

the real trouble
is the local Indians
don't know about our efforts
to keep this school decent

Painter

he wakes still drunk to toil
from underneath stiff blankets
puts the water on to boil
the hotplate still working
electricity not cut off yet

isn't surprised to find dirty gyprock
pieces dumped by the door, scraps he hauled home drunk
on which to lay down lines
of paint so thick with childhood
residential school memories
his wife has to scrape them away
with a pallet knife
before they harden hurtful
and unproductive

speaking of his wife: she wants the latest painting done
she's always afraid he'll choke
to death on his own vomit
before the last painting can be sold
to buy pampers and pay the electric bill

she has and she will
hold him in her arms all night
to protect him from himself

Drowning Girl

later she finds herself sitting small in front of the bank building on East Hastings noticing the leftover bodies of red cedar leaves that lie here and there across the sidewalk, residue from last fall, their brown skeletal impressions stain the pavement   down the hill she can see the sea   water surrounded by water   she's sitting on the cement   cup out for the panhandle   another drowning brown prairie girl broke on the street waiting for her boyfriend to come through with his promise

things that are small

egg
sperm
cells dividing
zygote
embryo

pennies
a zero, tacked on
the bottom line

a well-placed sigh
a one syllable reply
a question mark

silence and
a lie
as thin as an eyelash

Honour Song

rounds of words, long Cree vowels
                              pierce the air
like a layered collage
            the expressions overlap
                        one another

sounds of my blood
                  language
            blood memories dreaming through hands
that deliver a deliberate four-beat strike
                        pum
                        pum
                        pum
                        pum
each reverberates on the taut skin
of the drum, fine and tough

women sing their honour
                  high
until the generous spirit of the drum
enters my chest,
                  ripples to that dark centre
            where sweet notes fold over
                  and edge each other out
                              one
                              upon one
                              upon one
                              upon one

four rounds until
            the last strike leaves me
                        overflowing and clean

The Apology

you show up with your tight-lipped smile
hard to read, a red carnation at your breast
looks like stained tissue

you respond more to the cameras than the people
start and end by saying you're sorry, *offer an apology*
you say the hard facts while the soft ones
float in the background, inch around
the room, like a buffalo

soft facts like baby fat, like children's cheeks

not in so many words, but
the cult-quality photos tell a portion
of what there is to be remorseful for: not one fat child
                        for over a hundred years

and it's not just food
experiments in malnutrition
clothing and shelter denied, but
            the human stuff, what a child wants most—
                    affection, protection,
                            to belong—held

in the musty records
embraced between
the lines, the ratio of caregivers
to children leaves no room
for pity

all were deprived
children died

you sound sincere you slippery sweater-vested seal
man, less attractive version of yourself
so learn this, don't miss
the point:
an ending doesn't follow
a beginning
the story endures—

sixties-poached babies
learned to slide "birth family"
around on budding tongues
subtext: momma wasn't good enough
you *sowed these seeds* and you
apologize for having done this
thing that is still in the doing

our stolen women like prey: beautiful
Jane Doe at the bottom of a river
and no one's in charge or finds it strange
children grow up but keep dying
regrettably

a mother under a boil-water order
so long her babies all become adults
never knowing clean water
the order, still not lifted

education pushes Samuel out
of a seat not meant for an Indian graduate
he's learned well about your *legacy of problems*

no, ticklish man, *we are sorry*
doesn't drive a stake through the heart
of the monster with the bloody smile as you

pat your lips dry
with the bloom at your breast
    extraordinary resilience and courage
    doesn't close
    a sucking wound

Kohkum

I

and seven living children later
she walks out on him, slings their clothes,
dishes, even food into black garbage bags
they each carry something, even the little ones
toting their packages like babies in their arms

her back hurts to bend and lift
the second-youngest child when they reach the city
but she carries him anyway, until he feels
able to carry his swaddled package, until they find a place
as likely as any to stop and rest
the dusty north-central neighbourhood

one small howling dog—gristled meat, leashed
on a front lawn and Lorne, the boldest, on his knees to quiet
the animal before he slips the rope free
and the mutt follows him:
now they are one more mouth to feed

II

the footsteps of her boyfriends fall
loud in the hallway and the busted drywall sings
late-night tunes; one brings a record player, then
conveniently disappears so
Lorne moves it to the kids' room
and the scratched discs keep them
innocent, in high spirits

and she tells herself the city does her no harm
except her brother always says it's killing her
and will someday drive her children apart
and away, like fragments of a shattered cup

III

and still
in her dying she remembers
the spirit-well of home
and the mist like smoke rising
off the curved brush, the dry yellow dogwood
that dots the hills

and her kohkum's soft touch
against her hair, those hands bent and knowing
her neck thin, a delicate thing

Descended from Daybird

at the wake she sits
perched on her chair, attended
as an Elder should be
fine yellow skin, a fragile bloom
amongst the other kohkums
and moshums
spun of red silk
she is: first lady of the blue hills
from a clan name
wing-clipped to bird
made and marked just so:
narrow iron eyes reaching
into a look that scalds me red
fierce flare of the nostrils
she is: of bird women
as dainty as a dime,
tapered fingers pressed
to the breastbone

and another time, in the city,
my bandy-legged uncle laughs
head thrown back so you can see
all the way up his nostrils
two neat holes so black they say midnight
him and all bird men:
a wiry bundle
of cocksure nervous dash
gun-slinger certain

calling up Daybird
who stood tall atop the touchwood hills
daybreak at his back, his eyes
following the red belt line
Carleton Trail already broken
by steel tracks
the trade gone dry and white men
standing like sterile hunters
atop mountains
of bleached buffalo skulls

When Someone Remembers My Father

when someone remembers my father
it's always a gift

a cousin calls him Uncle Barry
she smiles at me when she says,
Uncle Barry was my favourite
and I fix on her words, charmed
someone remembers
and, she says,
Uncle Barry used to babysit me
I wish I could even be
jealous

because I can't remember
except through blood and bone
and the way my jaw calls up the shape of his
and the narrow set of dark eyes
the flash of anger
quick

he was wiry, a scrappy fighter
the night he died outside a bar
he fought the fuck out of them
fought like fuck, man
but died just the same

I wish I could take him back
adore him, my most favourite dad ever
and say, *gimme a drag of your cigarette*
tough guy
and he could say,
watch it, kid

Cloud Naming

Thirteen and mid-summer-bored you sit frog-legged on the grass face
to the sun and I push you over onto your back where we wrestle   my
reckless hot body pressed to you the skin of your arms, your strug-
gling biceps under my hands I hold you down at least I try... Our
families say we are like sisters and tempted   we let the idea draw
us along its slippery red path   make up scenarios to fill ourselves
with something that might be missing   secret sisters, lost siblings,
twins—one baby kidnapped and sold by baby traders passed from
hand to hand like a baton in a relay race   the myth works since we
are both yellow-tan, raven-eyed, dark-maned and mainly because one
of us is only a pretender: adopted

after a while we lie   side by side chewing stems staring into blue,
cloud naming, pointing "A dragon, see? See?" Creating something
out of thin air   talking out loud about nothing there's a tiny rain-
bow in one of the clouds   I see it first and you tell me it's a sign
of something   maybe good luck   small fortunes   which? I've
forgotten but a simple pleasure enters me   and even as the dragon
wool melts across the sky   I wish for it to stay

My Mother Raised Me

in the city we eat canned potatoes and once
a canned chicken from the corner store we walk to—
we have no car to get groceries—
baffling how there is a whole bird
in the tin can, but it's true
along with shiny jellied fat
and a lot of caramel-coloured liquid—

she doesn't mind touching it while I squeal at her elbow
with exaggerated revulsion, and so
with her fingers in the slimy chicken
she teaches me
to do the things mothers are expected to do

as for the men, the things I recall the most are
her careful preparations, my part to play:
to fasten a hook and eye at the nape of her neck
or a clasp on a thin bracelet

not one of the men rises to the bar to prove worthy
of that shy charm of hers,
her warm skin and trembling hands
gentle

it has a taste, the disappointment,
hers and mine, with all of them,
including my father, whom I loyally detest
on her behalf
mitigated now that his lungs heave
and eyes fail him, a blind man

and now that she is gone I can see
that my kindness to him takes nothing
away from her, after all

Taste

first we drink a whole bottle
of fisheye
cheap red measures dropped
between umber lips
our breath a little fast exhaling
a soft poison
in the trembling air
your laughter a sweet speedball
touch
and finally
after a long time we fall

on the bed
a second bottle between us
and I dare to slowly fold you
over on my palate
dance up and down ripe relief and dark scent
mixing you with the wine and spices
sweetgrass, oak, kinnikinnick
chokecherry paste and the curve of your brown hip
and when you ask me to put my tongue
on you it's the most truth I've ever heard
the air stands at attention as I ride over the cliff
and between the rise and fall
the moon makes a bet and the stars wink

the candle melts its wax down to a nub and
neither of us cares when its light goes out
fierce all night until we drift away
to sleep and wake in the daylight
to drink water and love again
and finally rise to eat and shower
and I lace my fingers into yours and you kiss me
in the street on the corner in front of the world
and I lick you from my lips like salt

Fruit

in youth it's true
fleshy pomegranate opens on your tongue
like a woman
red orbs to be sucked
                            to juice
and dribble down your chin

pulpy blueberry fingertips
caress your lips
and leave behind a smear
of watery wanting

sniff me, red berry
            the red of joy
raspberry basin a wet offering
seeds like little hairs
            in the teeth

ready tomatoes
            firm in your hands
b-size breasts of the fruit kingdom
your thumb
            stroking the firm skin
                        dreamy

            once, your rind was full
and plump like a new orange
to be taken for granted
for someone to caress and squeeze
            or not, what did you care? no need
            to vie for the attention you got

oh time, she's a dirty trick
you can do the math but none of it
                    adds up now
to the avocado, kiwi, cabbage
        day old fruit
        that's become of you

Hands

today you are an old man;
on the other side of the conversation
I once wished you destroyed. As a child

I worshipped your two small guns, polished
your boots with a series of wooden and black-bristled brushes,
much admired the intoxicating scent of the bootblack

my mother was always on edge
what was she so afraid of
whiskey breath and a rough touch, the guns,
someone who didn't love her back?

you breathe shallowly in your chair
perk up now and then to ask for your drink
then fall asleep for a minute
I touch your hand when it flops to my knee
notice your swollen knuckle at the base of your finger

you feel my grasp and your watery look
shifts to your hand in mine, puzzled—
how easy it is to slip away from ourselves
to where the familiar is unfamiliar

your hands are different now: relaxed, open,
not clenched in fists or raised to strike
you squeeze my fingers and
I make peace with the facts:

I've never once held your hand in affection
but instead, drank all the whiskey, straight and fast,
drawn to the cowboy's poison,
smoked the Export A greens, cared less

I've never once held your hand in affection
but I'm willing, now that we've settled on death
with our quasi-handshake, to take a second look—
to set aside old resentments, long as they are
so I can reassure you

it's all meant something—
I'm here to watch you die
but not before I hear you, witness
whatever comes next, as you close out

how heavy you look now, breathing
rough as if your chest tows you toward the ground
core pull of centre to centre—

here, now, I find I've softened
into a grudging love, a swaybacked pretending
I'm not angry anymore and I prop
your glass in your hand

there is everything left to be done

Mistress

hopeful pretender
wondrous
of things unearned
a mistress always comes

on white bread
she is delicious
sunshine

even when it rains
rubber boots or bare feet
in a mud puddle
warm and squishy

lost car keys
found, courage
girl scout badge
of boldness
peripheral
true love

and promises
lipstick-stained teeth
chipped nail polish
blue, nude
pantyhose and sandals
a red coat
purse with a cheap
gold clasp

a mistress never comes
cheap
red wine wanting
to breathe
no wait
make it
champagne
only the best
French restaurants
escargots and bonbons
for the lady
a real gold clasp

to snap a heart-clock
into her cheap red purse
the dream says:
Do Not Disturb

Sweep

I can hold in the palm of my right hand
all that I have left: one story-gift from an uncle,
a father's surname, treaty card, Cree accent echo, metal bits, grit—
and I will still have room to cock a fist

a given name buried deep
shared with sisters like baby-sleep, forgotten;
the daydream of the honour drum
a long-rhythm marrow strum

the story goes: in the morning my father put on his snowshoes
the ones he made of white ash and rawhide lacing
and followed the rabbit trails crisscrossing the frozen lake
while my mother watched him go

then one day he returned home to dance
his wiry body across my mother's
to conceive another girl-child in the spark
between the flood, share Christmas oranges,
roll her over on his tongue, court her across
the kitchen in a flurry of fiddle-jig love

when he slid away again across
the frozen waapus-pockmarked lake
just before spring breakup
the welfare lady came to claim
my mother's babies

that's the first time my mother
twirled away in a kind of madness
went on to birth more than one daughter,
spare parts, she gifted each the same name
so certain she'd never see any of them again

in the cold I bite my tongue hard
enough to bring tears to my eyes
as a way to cure the dry mouth feeling
and remind myself I am alive

even though they are all dead now
I have to live with the memory:
my uncle's handsome chestnut fingers
crooked to clear dirty leaves from the grave

and the question
what does it mean to be full of grace
to open oranges on your tongue
and make things out of your bare hands?

Cremation

first I stand beside your closed pine box its sharp edges
covered by a white woollen blanket
and through the shroud my fingers work
a rivet along the lid near where I imagine your hand to be—
your graceful tapered fingers

I'm aware of the funeral man waiting
ready to wheel you into the next room
it all seems to happen in stages, this death business
room to room to room—I remember them all

we come with you so you won't have to be alone

he offers that I might want to push the button,
tells me some Hindus and Sikhs desire a funeral pyre,
take cremation as a consolation and want to participate
I tell him we're not those kind of Indians,
then allow myself to laugh but he doesn't
so I stay on my side of the glass
while your body burns I hold tight to my boys'
hands and stare straight ahead as you rise to air
and become part of the atmosphere
part of the white and yellow-centred daisies you adored
the convincing scent of the lilacs, so brief in spring
the apple tree with its small sour apples
the blossoms of the crabapple in your backyard
in the front, the giant pine that you remembered
as a seedling—at the end these were your whole world
and I think you finally forgot about the rest of it—
the ways you'd been hurt, by men and children alike,
debts others owed you—as you turned inward
with the preoccupation of dying
well

we leave the crematorium, your smoke
filtered through the chimneys, lit
in cold February air and perfect sky-blue sky

I imagine you now, unfettered
limbs whole again, spine straight and true,
rising to walk lightly off the boat, your hand
in the captain's, stepping down
to a place where you can dance once more
in your pretty shoes with your delicate
feet and slender legs, yes,
dance on the graves of the dead bastards
the ones who have it coming because
if you don't, who will?

This Is a Surprise

I
the day you die will not be the first day

II
I've killed you before
counted you as dead
wished the worst
stood beside the car wreck
watched your twisted body
hustled off in a black zip-up bag
poked sharp pins into your
voodoo doll brain
dug the knife in deep enough
to hit bone
choked you on your own whiskey vomit
jabbed the needle in hard
gave you aids in the 80s
pushed you in front of a train
got a big gun and blasted you
bashed your skull with a crystal ashtray

III
remembered your words
buried them alongside you
end to end
every time
in a new fresh mound

IV

and the weirdest part?
we always forgave each other
always cast among the worms
our implements of slaughter

V

but this time, its not what you expect
it wasn't up to me after all
you've done yourself in

VI

curl your quaking fingers
shake your fist and curse
your spotty liver, yellow skin,
half-capacity lungs moist sponges,
circulation stopped below the knees
fuzzy thoughts, watery eyes
and the sharp pains in your chest

VII

I'm surprised that I'll miss
the way you thought you had me fooled
as you spun me in your arms
nearly burned me with the cigarette hanging from your lip
apologized
by snatching roses and wine from the air

Acknowledgements

I am ever grateful for family, friends, community. My first reader, Declan, and my immediate family must be recognized for tolerating my many absences in the name of art. Elizabeth Philips for your mentorship and teaching—I love learning and this was a steep curve for me. In the same vein I thank the many artists and writers who have inspired, encouraged and supported me as a writer over the years. Maarsii to my extended family members who provided me with information and initial research material, even though none of us would have guessed it would lead to a book of poetry. Gratitude to my relations, present, past and future, who help guide my spirit and intentions in a good way. The Saskatchewan Archives Board, Library and Archives Canada, the Anglican Archives, and archives in general deserve my praise and appreciation for preserving the records and making them available to researchers for a variety of purposes. Thank you to two important and vital institutions for art and culture, the Saskatchewan Arts Board and the Canada Council for the Arts, for financial support and encouragement. Most of all, love and honour to the children who attended Canada's residential schools, the survivors, and the ones who did not come home. We must never forget our shared history and legacy.